How to be Brilliant at

GRAMMAR

Brilliant Publications

We hope you and your class will enjoy using this book. Other books in the series include:

If you would like further information on these or other titles published by Brilliant Publications, write to the address given below.

Published by Brilliant Publications,
The Old School Yard, Leighton Road, Northall,
Dunstable, Bedfordshire LU6 2HA

Written by Irene Yates
Illustrated by Kate Ford

Printed in Great Britain by the Warwick Printing
Company Ltd

© Irene Yates 1993
ISBN 1 897675 02 X

First printed 1993
Reprinted 1994, 1997
10 9 8 7 6 5 4 3

Contents

Introduction

How to be Brilliant at Grammar contains 42 photocopiable ideas for use with 7-11 year olds. The book provides a flexible, but structured, resource for teaching children to understand and use parts of speech and punctuation.

The sheets are self-explanatory and ready to use; the only extra resources needed are a pen or pencil and perhaps some extra paper. The answer sheet on page 47 provides the answers to the puzzle activities.

In a way grammar is about the medium and the message. Whereas the focus in school English teaching during the last two or three decades has been to a large extent upon the message, in this book we focus on the medium.

Learning about grammar gives children the tools to be able to talk about and understand their language development. All words in a sentence can be divided according to their usage into eight different classes: nouns, pronouns, adjectives, verbs, adverbs, prepositions, conjunctions and interjections. A word which may ostensibly be the 'same' may have a very different meaning, according to its usage:

The *well* dried up. (noun)
I feel *well* today. (adjective)
The tears *well* in her eyes. (verb)
He plays *well*. (adverb)
Well – who would believe it? (interjection)
Girls, as *well* as boys, play football. (preposition)

(Current non-standard English also uses the word 'well' in an adjectival capacity, eg 'I was *well* pleased' – but although you can say 'the house was *well*-appointed', which also uses the word in an adjectival capacity, the first example is not good English.)

Looking at grammar necessitates taking the language apart and assessing it in little fragments. The difficulty for children is to see the words objectively, not as *meaning* in their communications, but as the functional nuts and bolts of writing and speaking. They have to be able to take one or two steps backwards from the message to be able to analyse the medium. Once the medium is understood, pupils will be able to use their knowledge of grammar and punctuation as tools to improve their own writing.

The **EXTRA!** boxes on each page provide opportunities for children to experiment with language and to apply what they have learned in a variety of contexts. These should be supplemented with other writing and speaking activities.

Links to the National Curriculum

The activities in *How to be Brilliant at Grammar* allow children to have opportunities to:

2. **Key skills**

c use punctuation marks correctly in their writing, including full stops, question and exclamation marks, commas, inverted commas, and apostrophes to mark possession.

d check spellings and meanings of words, using dictionaries where appropriate. When looking up words, pupils should be taught to apply their knowledge of initial and subsequent letters.

3. **Standard English and Language Study**

b develop their understanding of the grammar of complex sentences, including clauses and phrases. They should be taught how to use paragraphs, linking sentences together coherently. They should be taught to use the standard written forms of nouns, pronouns, verbs, adjectives, adverbs, prepositions, conjunctions and verb tenses.

c distinguish between words of similar meaning, to explain the meanings of words and to experiment with choices of vocabulary.

What's in a name?

Nouns are the names of things, places and people.

Your name_____is a noun. It is a proper noun. Proper nouns are 'real names' and they always start with a capital letter.

You are also:

| | a son |
| or | a daughter |

maybe	a brother
or	a sister
or	an only child

a pupil

a writer

Fill in as many nouns as you can to show who you are and what you do.

_____

_____

_____

_____

_____

_____

_____

Write here nouns of what you might be when you grow up.

_____

_____

_____

_____

_____

What is a noun?
N ames –
O rdinary
U sual
N o big deal!

EXTRA!
If you could be somebody else, who would you like to be? Write a story about how your life would be different.

Nouns are words which name things

Every person, place or thing has a name – a 'noun' that names it. You can usually put 'a' or 'an' in front of a noun, and it will make sense. For example: a space buggy, a rocket, a satellite, a space invader, an aeroplane.

Make a list here of 18 things you'd find on another planet. Some have been done for you:

1.   a crater
2.   a humanoid
3.   an android
4.
5.
6.

7.
8.
9.
10.
11.
12.

13.
14.
15.
16.
17.
18.

Colour in the nouns you can see in this picture.

EXTRA!
Make a list of all the nouns you've coloured in. Write a space story using them.

How to be Brilliant at Grammar

Name that place!

The names of places are 'nouns'. Look at the pictures. Decide what noun the picture is showing. Then write a sentence using the noun to explain what happens there.

An airport is where you go to catch a plane.

_____

_____

Draw your own pictures here.

The planet Zog is where the green eight-toed monster lives.

The Stegosaurus romps in the swamps.

EXTRA!

'Proper nouns' are 'real names' like your name is _____ .
They must always have capital letters to start them. Challenge your friend to write
a list of towns and countries. Who knows the most?

Pyramid busters

'Proper nouns' are proper names. They always begin with a capital letter.

Proper nouns can name:
people: Mr Rogers, Lucy, Mike Jones, Manjit Gill
places: New York City, London, Cornwall, Asia, Mars
things (like TV programmes, films or brand names):
          Neighbours, Brookside, Blockbusters, Snickers

Answer the questions on the Pyramid buster board. They are all proper nouns. Score three
points for every one you get right.

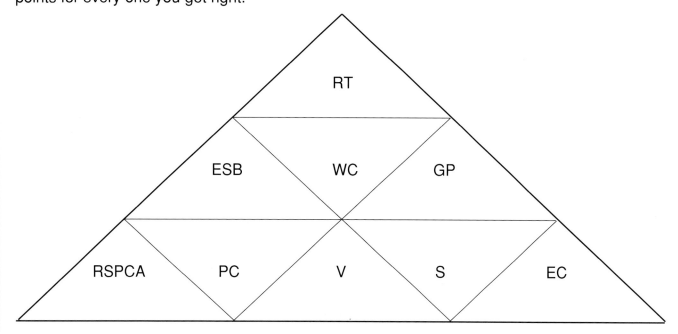

RT	What RT runs through London?
ESB	What ESB is the second tallest building in New York City?
WC	Which WC belonging to the Queen was badly burned in a big fire?
GP	Which GP might be your doctor?
RSPCA	What RSPCA looks after stray animals?
PC	Which PC is heir to the throne?
V	Which V is a planet in our solar system?
S	Which S is a country in southern Europe?
EC	Which EC is between England and France?

Teacher: see page 47 for answers.

EXTRA!
Trace the Pyramid buster grid on to a separate sheet and design a proper noun quiz.
Test a friend.

How to be Brilliant at Grammar

Acrostic puzzles

The answers to these puzzles are all nouns. You'll get the answer from the *last letter* of each word.

Remember, you'll get the answer from the LAST LETTER of the clues

A good fruit to eat

1. You use this to wash with
2. You need your eyes to do this
3. Something you can put up to keep off the rain
4. If you stroke a kitten it will do this

These make a good collection

1. You fasten your shirt up with these
2. Blow out the candles and make a
   _____
3. You swap
4. A kind of seabird
5. Belonging to the Middle Ages
6. Something girls wear

Use a dictionary to help you

Healthy to drink

1. When you illustrate something you
   _____
2. Found in a pod
3. You do this on a chair
4. To take no notice
5. Pretty plant

A small amphibian

1. _____ of bread
2. A meal
3. A greeting
4. A hen lays this

Teacher: see page 47 for answers.

EXTRA!
Make up four acrostic puzzles and swap with a friend.
Make the answers nouns or adjectives (words which describe things).
Try longer words. How long a word can you make a puzzle for?

How to be Brilliant at Grammar

The amazing plural machine

If you have one of something, the noun is singular. If you have more than one, it's plural. Usually you just need to add an 's' to make a noun plural, but there are some exceptions to the rule. This flow chart will help you to remember them.

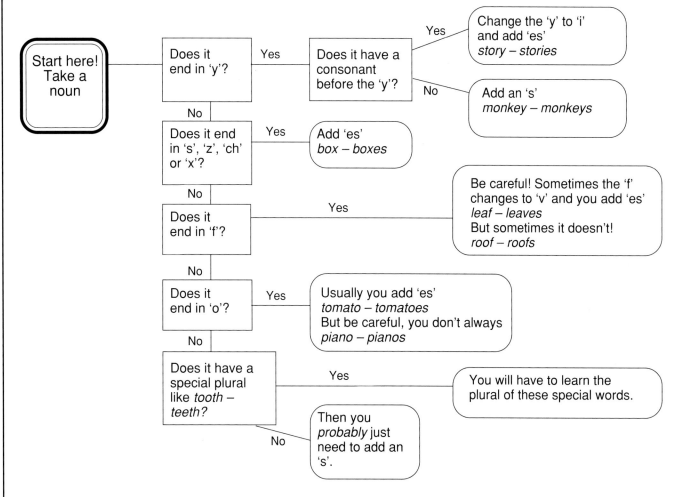

Use a dictionary to find out the plurals of these words:

toy	berry	shoe
potato	ox	fox
man	comic	wish
movie	goose	diary
bus	hoof	mouse

EXTRA!
What would you call a small amount or one piece of each of these?
Rain, dust, straw, butter, bread, tea, sugar, wind, paper.

Collective nouns

'Collective nouns' are nouns that give a name to a group of people, animals or things. Some collective nouns for animals you might know are:

a swarm of bees
a flock of sheep
a drove of cattle
a herd of deer
a shoal of fish
a school of porpoises
a plague of locusts

But do you know these:

a crash of rhinoceroses
a kindle of kittens
a peep of chickens
a skulk of foxes
a sloth of bears
a troop of monkeys
a watch of nightingales
a knot of toads
a mumble of moles

Make up your own collective nouns for:

teachers   friends

school children   swimmers

joggers   computer games

caravans   supermarket trolleys

disc jockeys   mountain bikes

EXTRA!
How do you think the real collective nouns were created? Talk about the words
and try to work out how they came into being. Make a book about collective nouns.
Illustrate it with cut-out pictures and your own drawings.

How to be Brilliant at Grammar

Getting rid of nouns

You can't always refer to something by using the noun for it – the nouns clutter sentences up. For instance:

The dragon is breathing fire through the dragon's nostrils.   would be better as   The dragon is breathing fire through *its* nostrils.

The words we use instead of nouns are called 'pronouns'. Here are some to learn:

I   me   you   she   he   it   her   him   we   us   they   them

This story doesn't have any pronouns. Read it aloud with a friend and try to spot where you could replace nouns with pronouns.

Help! The dragon is coming!

The dragon slithered down the street with flames curling from the dragon's nostrils.

'Help!' shouted Chris. 'The dragon's coming and the dragon's going to set fire to the school and the school will go up in flames! The fire will be a disaster!'

The children peered through the windows. The dragon came menacingly on. The children saw the dragon breathing more fire.

'Whoosh!' the dragon went, 'Whoosh! Whoosh!'

The children began to scream but Chris knew just what to do. 'Direct the dragon to the swimming pool!' Chris shouted. 'We'll try to get the dragon to the water. Then the fire will go out!' Chris and the teachers and the children and the police and the people who were watching followed Chris's plan. The plan worked.

Chris became a hero.

Write the story again here, using pronouns. Be careful though, if you use too many pronouns the story will be confusing.

Run out of space? Use the back of the sheet!

EXTRA!

Take a story from a book. Read it aloud to your friend, but change all the pronouns to nouns and listen to how it sounds. Get your friend to guess the pronouns that should be there and list them on a piece of paper; then check together.

How to be Brilliant at Grammar

Lots of action

A sentence needs lots of action.

Sentences get their action from the words we call 'verbs'. Sometimes verbs are called *doing* or *being* words.

A sentence without a verb is:

Just a banana!

An unusual hat!

A dog's bone!

That stupid programme!

With a verb the sentence might be:

I *will have* just a banana!

He *is wearing* an unusual hat.

We *dug* up a dog's bone.

I'*m not watching* that stupid programme.

Write six incomplete sentences here:

Write six proper sentences here:

EXTRA!
Try to have a conversation with a friend without using any verbs.

How to be Brilliant at Grammar

14

Loads of verbs

Everybody in this picture is doing something. There are lots of verbs here!

Write the story of everything you can see happening in this picture, then go back and circle all the verbs that you can find in your story.

Verbs DO!
Verbs ARE!
A sentence without one
Won't go far!

If you run out of space, use the back of the sheet.

EXTRA!
Choose a story from a book and read it carefully. How many verbs can you find?
Make a list of at least 50! There are other verbs than 'doing' words.
Are is one, and *was* and *have* and *must* and *should* and *am*. These are verbs of
'being' and 'having'. Are there any in your story?

Past, present and future

You have to change verbs to show whether their actions happened in the past, are happening now, or will happen in the future. This is called changing the 'tense' of the verb. You probably say the verb tenses properly without thinking about them, because that's how you learned to talk. But you have to think about them more when you're writing.

Put the sentences from the speech bubbles into the right boxes.

Past

Present

Future

Adjectives describe things

'Adjectives' are words which describe nouns; they describe something or someone.

Work with a friend. Draw your friend on this page and write 10 adjectives to describe her or him. Do you agree with your partner's description of you?

Adjectives are nice 'n' easy
Or difficult,
Or bad,
Or squeezy,
Or breezy,
Or cheesy,
Or ...

EXTRA!
Draw yourself, or someone in your family, and write 20 adjectives to fit that person.

How to be Brilliant at Grammar

Find the adjectives

All the words in the word search are adjectives. They all begin with the letter 'a'. They describe:

a boat drifting

a raft floating

a house blazing

a sky glowing

something living

someone sleeping

a door not properly closed

someone frightened

someone by themselves

Words can go backwards or forwards and up or down.

```
A  F  R  A  I  D  S  T  A
J  O  T  F  I  R  D  A  L
A  A  S  L  E  E  P  G  I
R  A  L  O  N  E  G  L  V
A  B  L  A  Z  E  T  O  E
P  S  E  T  A  W  A  W  T
```

Write the words you have found here:

EXTRA!
Challenge your friend.
Choose another letter
of the alphabet and give
your friend 20 minutes
to create a word search with
six adjectives. Can you
find the words in less
than 5 minutes?

Tongue-twisting adjectives

Can you say these quickly? Practise with a friend.

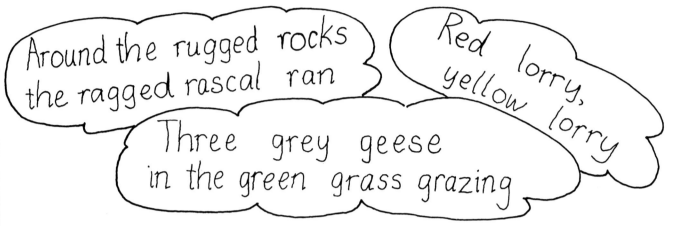

Around the rugged rocks the ragged rascal ran

Red lorry, yellow lorry

Three grey geese in the green grass grazing

Each sentence has two adjectives. Circle them when you find them.

Make up five tongue twisters of your own. The rule is: each must have at least two adjectives. Test them on your friend. Have fun!

EXTRA!
Make a list of six adjectives and then make up six tongue twisters using them.

How to be Brilliant at Grammar

Adjectives chart

Fill in the adjectives to go with the nouns, using the letters at the top of the column as the initial letters. Use a dictionary or thesaurus to help you find your words.

	S	M	A	R	T
family	small	messy	active	rich	trendy
playtime					
homework					
computer					
weekend					
holiday					
school					

Draw a picture here of the small, messy, active, rich and trendy family.

EXTRA!
Describe a spider. Search for an adjective for each letter of the alphabet that could describe a spider. Try to make it funny.

Comparing things

How do you compare? Fill in the spaces with words and pictures.
These words are called 'comparative adjectives'.

I've got a hairy spider.

I've got a hairier one.

I've got the hairiest spider!

That's the ugliest mutant I've ever seen!

My haircut is spikier than yours.

My trainers are smelly.

Can you do this one?   (Hint: it's *not* good, gooder, goodest!)

I'm good at grammar.

EXTRA!
Think of six adjectives. Test a friend on the
comparative adjectives.

How to be Brilliant at Grammar

Tell me more

You get lots of help from 'adverbs' when you're writing because they're the words that tell you exactly how, when, where or why something happens.

The easiest adverbs to identify are the ones that end with 'ly' – but not all of them do!

You could write a story without any adverbs. For example:

Marty was left to look after his little brother, James. James played with his toys. Marty wanted fun. He figured if James kept busy, what could go wrong? Marty sneaked out of the kitchen door...

With adverbs it's better. The adverbs are circled. The arrows show which words they modify.

When Marty was left to look after his little brother, James played happily with his toys. Marty wanted some fun. He figured if James played busily, what could go wrong? Sneakily, Martin crept out of the kitchen door and ...

Write what happened next. Use these adverbs:

only	accidentally	softly
very	too	angrily
naughtily	almost	desperately
quickly		

Run out of space? Use the back of the sheet.

EXTRA!
With a friend, choose a favourite story from the library and search for adverbs.
Find 10 and use them to write your own story.

How to be Brilliant at Grammar

Be a word magician!

Change an adjective into an adverb with a simple wave of your pencil!

Adjectives (words describing nouns) can be turned into adverbs (words describing verbs) as easily as pie. This trick gives you another way of writing (or saying) a sentence that basically means the same thing.

The *greedy* dog scoffed the sausages.   could become

The dog scoffed the sausages *greedily*.

Make up sentences for these adjectives:

rough   loud

cosy   noisy

equal   terrible

sensible   joking

With one wave of your magic pencil change the adjectives into adverbs. Write your new sentences here:

> ## EXTRA!
> Watch your spelling:
> - Some adjectives already end in 'y' (easy, heavy, lucky). What happens to them?
> - Some adjectives end with an 'e' that you have to lose (gentle, true, humble).
> - Some adjectives end with 'ful' (truthful, careful, thankful). What happens to them?

How to be Brilliant at Grammar

Little words

Prepositions are the kind of little words you use all the time without thinking. They tell you, generally, where and what.

Some prepositions are:

off	across	into	in	over
behind	under	before	on	near
at	after	by	to	because

Write a funny story using as many prepositions as you can. Take for your story-line the famous Humpty Dumpty. Make it modern, make it funny. Underline all the prepositions you've used. Give yourself three points for each one you've used.

How many points did you get?

EXTRA!
Read your story aloud to a friend. Play spot the prepositions.
Give two points for each one spotted.

It's a whole sentence!

A sentence isn't a sentence unless it has a verb in it. You can put a noun and a verb together to make a whole, proper sentence that only has two words. For example:

Ducks quack.

Children play.

Fish swim.

Write two sentences with only two words.

_____

_____

Write two sentences with three words.

_____

_____

Write two sentences with four words.

_____

_____

_____

Write two sentences with five words.

_____

_____

What's the shortest sentence you can write?

_____

What's the longest sentence you can write with only one verb? Make sure it makes sense!

_____

_____

_____

_____

_____

EXTRA!
Challenge your friend to a contest.
Who can write the most two
word sentences?

How to be Brilliant at Grammar

Matching verbs

Verbs always have to match the rest of the sentence. The verb 'to be' is an easy one to learn by heart.

I am   We are
You are   They are
He is
She is

When talking about things that happened in the past you need to use the past tense:

I was   We were
You were   They were
She was
He was

If you remember this by heart, you won't make mistakes such as 'They WAS going to the park.'

I thought they WERE going swimming...

The verbs in these sentences don't match the rest of the sentence. What's wrong with them? Write the correct sentences.

He's fell in the pond.

Who done that?

I swimmed six lengths.

She drawed a helicopter.

The ship sunk.

We begun yesterday.

They wondered if he were going with them.

EXTRA!
Write a story about your day, making sure *all* the verbs are absolutely right.

How to be Brilliant at Grammar

Subjects and verbs

The subject (the who) and the verb (the action word) always
have to 'agree' in a sentence.

Circle the correct sentences:

The aliens go shopping on Saturday.	The alien and the monster is having a fight.
The aliens goes shopping on Saturday.	The alien and the monster are having a fight.
The monster does the housework.	We were watching the space film.
The monster do the housework.	We was watching the space film.
The rocket go to the moon.	I like to play games on my computer.
The rocket goes to the moon.	I likes to play games on my computer.

Choose from each pair of words. Write *one* sentence where the subject and verb agree.

say, says

make, makes

take, takes

are, is

have, has

like, likes

put, puts

were, was

EXTRA!
Write a story about a monster and an alien making friends.
Make sure your subjects and verbs agree.

Subjects and predicates

Proper sentences have two parts: a subject and a predicate.

- The *subject* is the person, thing or place written or spoken about.

- The *predicate* is what is said or written about the subject.

Look at these sentences:

Subject	Predicate
The girl	went to school.
Mum	packed her lunch-box.
The dog	ran after her.
It	grabbed the lunch-box from her bag.
The girl	had nothing to eat!

Add your own predicates to continue the story:

The teacher   _____

They both   _____

The sandwiches   _____

The girl   _____

The dog   _____

Add your own subjects to finish the story.

_____ said, 'I definitely packed them.'

_____ was nowhere to be seen.

_____ was a complete mystery.

EXTRA!
Make a game with a partner. Use 10 pieces of card each. One writes subjects
on their cards and the other writes predicates. Take the cards at random,
one from each pile, to see what funny sentences you get.

Spot the sentence

Sentences make sense. They might be short, they might be long – but they *always* make sense. If they don't, they're just *not* sentences!

Phrases are groups of words, without a verb, that don't make any sense at all, unless they're part of a sentence. Look at these sentences and phrases:

My puppy

In a kennel

Lots of exercise

My puppy is called Fred

Fred sleeps in a kennel

Fred gets lots of exercise

It's easy to pick out the phrases from the sentences here!

Use the theme of a new puppy to write a story. Make a list of phrases first as notes to help you. Then write the story in proper sentences.

If you run out of space use the back of the sheet.

EXTRA!
Remember, you can probably join some of your sentences together to make them longer. Use conjunctions to join them (such as *and, but, after, before, as, since*). Rewrite your story using conjunctions. Put some adverbs and adjectives in as well. Read your list of phrases aloud to a friend. Then read your complete story. Which sounds best?

Lots of clauses

Clauses are groups of words in a sentence. Each clause in a sentence has a verb. The *main clause* in a sentence makes sense all by itself, but the *subordinate clause* doesn't.

Main clause
The pop-star sang her latest hit

Subordinate clause
when the audience called for her.

'The pop-star sang her latest hit' could be a sentence by itself, but 'when the audience called for her' couldn't.

Split these sentences into main clauses and subordinate clauses. Be careful! The main clause doesn't always come first. It may even be split up.

She sang as the audience roared.

The concert was a sell-out because she was top of the pops.

As they left the concert everybody cheered.

The singer who had the most hits was the star of the show.

She signed autographs all night because the fans kept knocking on her door.

The pop-star won a golden album when her song reached number one.

Main clause	**Subordinate clause**

Teacher: see page 47 for answers.

EXTRA!
With a friend, choose a page in a book and look for sentences with one main clause and more than one subordinate clause. Remember, each clause will have a verb.

Back to front and inside out

Do you know the alphabet the right way round, back to front, inside out and upside down?

The right way round's easy:

a b c d e f g h i j k l m n o p q r s t u v w x y z

Copy it out to make sure you know it the right way round.

_____

Back to front? Cover up the top and bottom of the page and write it back to front here:

_____

Inside out? Look at the pattern on the snail, it starts in the middle with A. Four more letters are given – fill in the rest of the pattern to get to Z.

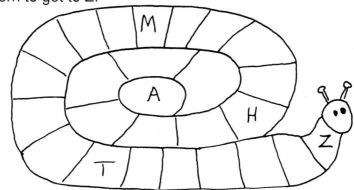

> **The alphabet –**
> Keeping order is
> as easy as ABC!

Upside down? Mirror the letters on the bottom line.

a b c d e f g h i j k l m n o p q r s t u v w x y z

_____

_____

EXTRA!
To make an ABC book, take two sheets of paper. Put them one on top of the other.
Fold them in half. Cut across the fold. Fold in half again. Cut across the fold.
Fold in half again and staple in the centre. Mark each page with a letter of the alphabet.
Use your book to collect words and spellings.

How to be Brilliant at Grammar

Advertise yourself

Look at the advertisements in a newspaper.
See how many adjectives you can find.

Advertise yourself, using adjectives only,
beginning at A and going through to Z.

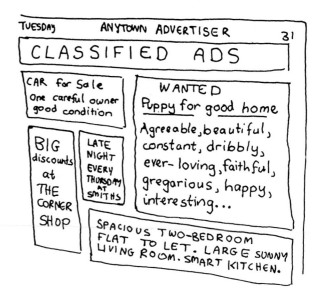

A

B

C

D

E   P

F   Q

G   R

H   S

I   T

J   U

K   V

L   W

M   X

N   Y

O   Z

EXTRA!
Make up a sentence using at least 10 words beginning with the same letter.
For example: Baby bunnies bound by, brightly bouncing beside big black burrows.
Use a dictionary to help you.

Put it in order

This story is all mixed up. Work with a friend to get it right. Cut out the strips and paste them in the proper order on a separate sheet.

The children decided they would leave the mice alone after all.

There were seven babies nestling in the tin.

'It wouldn't be right, would it?' Jo answered anxiously.

Jo and her friend, Rashed, were playing cricket in the field.

'The mum's frightened,' Jo said.

In an old cardboard box, full of rubbish, there was a rusty paint tin.

The ball went zooming over the hedge.

Jo shouted, 'Hey, Rashed! Come and see what I've found!'

They both squeezed through a hole in the bushes.

'Cor!' said Rashed, 'shall we take them to school?'

The ball was nowhere to be seen, but Jo found something much more interesting.

Beside it was a little mouse, squeaking for all it was worth.

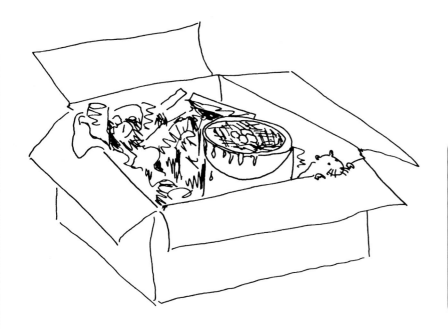

EXTRA!
Write your own story about an animal in the wild. Then cut up the sentences, muddle them up and give them to a friend to paste in the right order.

The brilliant memory trick

Use the alphabet to help you train your memory.

Say you want to remember six things:
* to post a letter
* to watch your favourite programme
* to phone your gran
* to fetch your comic from the newsagents
* to do your homework
* to clean your bedroom

Take the first six letters of the alphabet

A   B   C   D   E   F

Choose a theme. For example, animals:

For				**Imagine:**
A	have	Ant		An ant posting a letter
B		Butterfly		A butterfly switching on the TV
C		Cow		A cow talking on the phone
D		Dog		A dog eating a comic
E		Elephant		An elephant doing your homework
F		Fox		A fox putting your clothes away

Go through the alphabet, and hey presto! Remember your list!

Make a list of six items you want to buy. Link them to the alphabet pictures. Try again with the next six letters of the alphabet.

EXTRA!
Amaze your relatives with your memory. Start with 6, then 10, then 15, then 20, then 26 items. Get a friend to test you!

Make sense of this!

This story has 9 full stops and 11 capital letters missing. Put them where they belong.

you wouldn't believe a lion came from the same family of animals as a little cat, but it does there are other wild animals that belong to the cat family too these animals can be very dangerous usually they live in the wild, mostly in africa, though you can find lions in one part of india they live on the flesh of other wild animals such as zebra, wild pig or buffalo lions hunt in groups by day and night a group of lions is called a pride the male lion has a mane and he's much bigger and heavier than the female young lions are called cubs and they are as playful as little kittens

Draw a picture to go with the story.

New sentence?

Cap it, Al!

EXTRA!
Write your own lion story using these words: mane, claws, prey, pounce, hungry, savage, fierce, hunt, dangerous, play, caught. Use 15 full stops and 16 capital letters.

How to be Brilliant at Grammar

When is it a capital?

You already know some places where you need to use a capital, like for the word 'I' and at the beginning of a sentence. But do you know the other times when you must use capital letters? Write three examples underneath each one. Remember to use capital letters!

People's names

_____

_____

_____

Names of places

_____

_____

_____

Titles of books, plays, songs, newspapers, films and poems

_____

_____

Days of the week, months of the year, special days

_____

_____

Titles (such as President)

_____

_____

Titles before names (such as Prince, Lord)

_____

_____

Starting each new line of an address (write yours here):

_____

_____

_____

Names of streets, roads and buildings

_____

_____

You also need to use a capital letter when you write the name of God, Jesus Christ, Allah and words relating to them (such as Our Father).

EXTRA!
The other place you might find capitals is beginning each line of a poem.
Write a poem about a person or place you really like, starting each line with a capital letter.

What's going on?

How can you find out what's going on here? By asking questions, of course. Each question needs a question mark at the end of it. Why? Because it does!

Study the picture and write 16 sentences about it. Most should be questions, but some may be statements. Cross out a question mark each time you use one. How many are left?

?   ?

?   ?

?   ?

?   ?

?   ?

?   ?

?   ?

?   ?

EXTRA!

Compare your questions with a friend's. Swap papers and answer each other's questions.

How to be Brilliant at Grammar

Alien questions

These are the alien's answers.
What do you think are the
earthling's questions?

I have five.

From Mars.

By saucer.

Anything, I'm starving.

Yes.

No.

What do you think I am?

Is it a question, Mark?

EXTRA!
With a partner, make up a set of questions and answers between you.
Every question must be answered by another question. Can you do this?

How to be Brilliant at Grammar

Coping with commas

There are lots of different rules for commas. One of them is that commas always go into lists so that the words don't go running on and crash into each other. You need gaps between the words, just like you need gaps between cars on a motorway.

You can list as many things as you like in a sentence. The last item in the list should have 'and' in front of it. You don't need to put a comma in front of 'and'.

For example:

> For my birthday what I really want is a video game, a mountain bike, a camcorder, a pair of trainers, a pet snake, a TV for my bedroom, a computer and an underwater watch

> Before you get anything I'd like you to clean your teeth, comb your hair, dry the dishes, sort out your socks, phone your grandad, do your homework and muck out your bedroom!

Do some list conversations here, using commas.

> A comma is the pause button of a sentence.

Here are some ideas to help you: things in your desk, things in your school-bag, things you like about somebody, things you hate doing, what you like to eat, what you do at weekends and where you go for holidays. *Don't forget the commas!*

EXTRA!
Make up two lists without using commas.
Get a friend to put the commas in.

How to be Brilliant at Grammar

Commas and conjunctions

You can often join two sentences together to make them into one by using little words that we call 'conjunctions'. Conjunctions are a bit like bridges.

Here are some conjunctions:

but   so   or   either   and   neither   for   if

If you use these words to bridge two sentences, then you must use a comma before them.
Like this:

> We went to the burger bar, but there were massive queues.
>
> Dad said, 'No fries!', so I had two burgers instead!
>
> Should I have cheese on them, or not?
>
> I couldn't decide between cola or milk shake, either would do.

Finish the rest of the story yourself, using the conjuctions that are left.

Write another story on the back of the sheet, using all of the conjunctions.

Apostrophes

Read this story:

Sophie opened the cupboard in the kitchen belonging to her grandmother to find the dog biscuits that belonged to Ben. She looked for the dish belonging to Ben to put the biscuits in, but could only find a bowl belonging to the cat. 'That'll have to do,' she thought. She tipped the packet of biscuits belonging to Ben into the bowl belonging to the cat and called the name belonging to the dog through the kitchen door. In the garden belonging to her grandmother the cat pricked up the ears belonging to it. It had heard the rattle of the bowl belonging to it and rushed into the kitchen. Sophie placed the bowl belonging to the cat with the biscuits belonging to the dog on the kitchen floor and called Ben again. The dog raced in and went for the bowl belonging to the cat but the cat arched the back belonging to it and hissed at the dog. The dog scuttled out of the kitchen door with the tail belonging to it between the legs belonging to it!

What a mouthful! It would be much easier to read if it had apostrophes! An apostrophe looks like a comma, but it's used at the top of the letters. It shows you who owns what.

Sophie's pencil   The apostrophe shows you the pencil belongs to Sophie.
Ben's dog biscuits   The apostrophe shows you the dog biscuits belong to Ben.

With some small words you don't have an apostrophe: *its*, *his*, *hers*, *ours*, *yours*.

Write the story again here, with apostrophes:

Sophie opened the cupboard in her grandmother's kitchen...

If you run out of space, use the back of the sheet.

EXTRA!
Make up a story without apostrophes for a friend to put right! Have fun!

Contractions

When you're talking, you use contractions all the time without even knowing it. A contraction is when you fit two words together and make them sound like one. To write them down, you have to use an apostrophe where you've missed the letters out.

Write what these contractions stand for. Use the clues at the bottom of the page to help you.

I'm   who's

I've   we're

I'd   hasn't

she's   aren't

she'd   you've

you're   you'd

we've   shouldn't

it's   couldn't

haven't   wouldn't

weren't

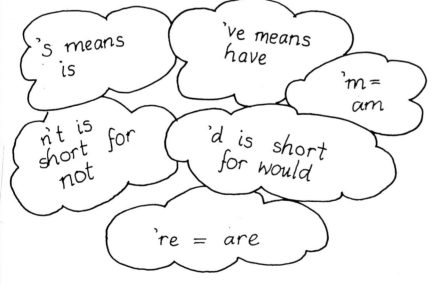

's means is

've means have

'm = am

n't is short for not

'd is short for would

're = are

Contractions
Lose a letter (or two) –
Gain an apostrophe!

These three are tricky because the words actually change:

shan't =   shall not

won't =   will not

can't =   can not

EXTRA!
Discuss what you did at playtime with a friend. Every time you use a contraction, mark it down on a piece of paper. How many contractions have you used?

Hyphens

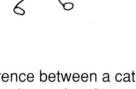

Q: What's the difference between a man eating dinosaur and a man-eating dinosaur?

A: A hyphen!

Q: What's the difference between a walking stick and a walking-stick?

A: A hyphen!

Q: What's the difference between a cat hunting mouse and a cat-hunting mouse?

A: A hyphen!

When you use a hyphen like this you have made a 'compound word'.

With a friend, make up some hyphenated compound word jokes of your own.

EXTRA!
Draw pictures to go with your jokes.

How to be Brilliant at Grammar

Inverted commas

Inverted commas are written at the top of the writing line. Sometimes they are called 'speech marks' because they come before and after speech. Like this:

Muhammad said, 'Hi! How are you today?'

In some books they are double like this:

"I'm fine, thanks," Jean answered. "How are you?"

You put what people are saying *inside* the inverted commas. They work exactly like speech bubbles in a cartoon, where the speech is always *inside* the bubbles. Don't put them around the bits that aren't spoken like: *he said, she said, I shouted, they whispered.*

The speech marks have been left out of this story. Read it carefully. Decide which bits someone is saying. When you're sure you're right, put the speech marks in.

It's a castle! Rashed said. A medieval castle!

And look! cried Emma, there's the Baron with his men getting ready to attack!

If they see us we'll be in trouble, Rashed whispered. Get down behind these trees. Somehow we've got to get across that moat and into the castle, but how are we going to do it?

Emma thought for a moment, then she said, The only thing I can think of is swimming across the moat and hiding underneath the bridge. The next time it's let down we might be able to hang on and sneak in some how.

It's going to be very dangerous, Rashed said. We might get caught and then what?

EXTRA!
Finish the story. What's going to happen when Emma and Rashed get into the medieval castle? And *how* did they get there in the first place?

Writing down speech

There are two ways of writing what somebody says:

Direct speech
'I love maths and science,' says Beth.

Direct speech uses the person's exact words.

Indirect speech
Beth says that she loves maths and science.

Indirect speech uses your own words.

Read this story. Some of it is written in direct speech, some in indirect speech.

Direct speech

1. 'We're going shopping,' said Mum.

3. Dad said, 'You'll do as you're told.'
4. 'But it's not fair!' Tom cried.

Indirect speech

2. Tom said he didn't want to go.

5. Dad didn't care whether it was fair or not. Tom couldn't stay at home by himself.

Follow the rest of the story. Tick the correct columns to show which sentences are written in direct speech and which are written in indirect speech.

	Direct speech	Indirect speech
'I always have to do things I don't want to do,' grumbled Tom.		
'Tough!' said Dad.		
Mum interrupted to tell them the bus was due at the corner in five minutes, so they'd better get their skates on.		
'Cheer up!' Dad said, 'You never know, we might have to walk by the bike shop.'		
Perhaps it wouldn't be so bad. Tom grinned and said he'd changed his mind. Maybe shopping was a good thing to do on Saturdays after all.		

On the back of the sheet, see if you can rewrite the story by swapping the direct speech to indirect and the indirect to direct.

> **EXTRA!**
> Write a scene for a play in script form.
> Swap with a friend and write the scene as
> a story with direct and indirect speech.

Guess what these are!

Work out the answers to the clues. They are all punctuation marks and the number of letters in each word is given in parentheses. When you have finished, fit the answers into the grid.

This one gives a long pause (4,4)

This one goes into a list and makes a short pause (5)

This one follows a surprise or a shout (11,4)

This one comes at the end of a question (8,4)

These are used for direct speech (8,6)

This one is used to show that something belongs to somebody (10)

This one shortens two words to one (11)

This comes at the beginning of a sentence or a proper name (7,6)

This one joins two words together to make a compound word (6)

How to be Brilliant at Grammar

Answer sheet

page 9
RT — River Thames
ESB — Empire State Building
WC — Windsor Castle
GP — General Practitioner
RSPCA — Royal Society for the Prevention of Cruelty to Animals
PC — Prince Charles
V — Venus
S — Spain
EC — English Channel

page 10
PEAR   soaP, seE, umbrellA, purR

SHELLS   buttonS, wisH, exchangE, gulL, medievaL, dresS

WATER   draW, peA, siT, ignorE, floweR

FROG   loaF, dinneR (or suppeR), hellO, egG

page 18

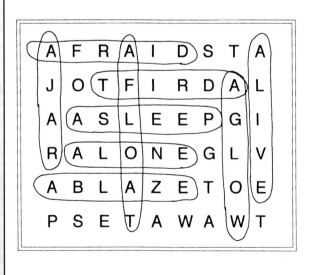

page 30

Main clause	Subordinate clause
She sang	as the audience roared
The concert was a sell-out	because she was top of the pops
Everybody cheered	as they left the concert
The singer was the star of the show	who had the most hits
She signed auto-graphs all night	because the fans kept knocking on her door
The pop-star won a golden album	when her song reached number one

page 46

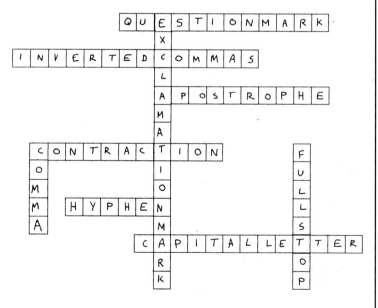

© Irene Yates
This page may be photocopied for use in the classroom only.

How to be Brilliant at Grammar

47

Glossary

adjective
Words used to describe things, people and events. For example: *brilliant* book, *tidy* classroom.

adverb
Words used to qualify the verb in the sentence, telling how, when and where. For example: ran *quickly*, wrote *when* necessary.

apostrophe
Punctuation mark with two uses:
a) shows who owns what: Ben's coat, the lady's hat.
b) for filling in where letters or figures are missing: don't, haven't, class of '93.

capital letter
Upper case letters used to start a sentence, or for a proper noun.

clause
Part of a sentence that has a verb. A *main clause* is a group of words with a verb, in a sentence, that makes complete sense. A *subordinate clause* is a group of words with a verb, in a sentence, that does not make sense without the main clause.

comma
Punctuation mark which gives a pause. It's used to separate two words, or groups of words in a sentence, to make the meaning clear.

compound word
Two or more words joined together; they can be nouns or adjectives. For example: water-wheel, six-ton elephant.

conjunction
The joining words in long sentences.

direct speech
The exact words that someone speaks.

exclamation mark
Punctuation mark used at the end of a sentence or a phrase to show great emotion.

full stop
Punctuation mark to make a long pause. Used at the end of sentences which are statements (whenever a question mark or exclamation mark isn't used).

hyphen
Punctuation mark used to link two words together to make one.

noun
A naming word.

phrase
A small group of words (without a verb) that isn't a complete sentence.

preposition
Words that put relationship into a sentence. For example: The dust *in* the road *from* the farm *to* the village was settled *by* the rain *in* the evening.

pronoun
Word used instead of a noun. For example: *her, she, his, him.*

question mark
Punctuation mark used at the end of a sentence which asks a question.

reported speech
Repeating or reporting, in different words, what someone has said.

sentence
A group of words which make complete sense on their own. Sentences always have a verb.

speech marks
Punctuation marks used to show exactly the words that someone has spoken. Sometimes they are called 'inverted commas'.

verb
A word which shows some action. For example: *run, jump, think, says.* There are also 'being' and 'having' verbs such as *was, is, were, has.*